DISCUSSION PAPER 64

I0122933

DEMOCRATIC GOVERNANCE
AND ACCOUNTABILITY IN AFRICA
In Search of a Workable Framework

ADEBAYO O. OLUKOSHI

NORDISKA AFRIKAINSTITUTET, UPPSALA 2011

Indexing terms:
Africa
Political development
Democratization
Political pluralism
Political reform
Democracy
Governance
Institutional framework
Constitutions

*The opinions expressed in this volume are those of the author
and do not necessarily reflect the views of Nordiska Afrikainstitutet.*

Language checking: Peter Colenbrander

ISSN 1104-8417

ISBN 978-91-7106-701-2

© The author and Nordiska Afrikainstitutet 2011

Production: Byrå4

Print on demand, Lightning Source UK Ltd.

Contents

Foreword

This Discussion Paper is based on the keynote address given by Professor Olukoshi at the inception workshop of the NAI Research Cluster on Conflict, Displacement and Transformation in October 2010. It provides an insightful exploration of democratic governance and accountability in Africa based on a radical and dialectical reading of the trends on the continent in the past two decades. It provides a critical analysis of the momentum for political reform and change on the continent, paying particular attention to the domestic and external sources of the pressures for change. The analysis draws on history to explain how, after independence, multiparty democracy gradually gave way to single party or military rule, as the party in power or regime squeezed out diversity or oppositional groups from the political space, often justifying such actions on the basis of the need to avoid distractions in the quest for an integrated and united political order and accelerated national development. The exclusion of marginalised groups and minorities constituted one of the early sources of domestic pressure for change. Another factor relates to the ways social contradictions linked to deepening economic crisis and its exacerbation by the IMF/World Bank structural adjustment programmes. All of these fed domestic pressures for democratisation, and eventually culminated in the 1990s in multipartyism. The paper then interrogates multipartyism/electoral pluralism as a basis for understanding democracy and democratic accountability in Africa. It is argued that the dominant neo-patrimonialism paradigm that results in a pessimistic reading of Africa's democratisation is "omnibus" and overly deterministic, tending to view everything through a single lens and leading to an analytical dead-end. The paper is also critical of the ways in which the concept of governance has been instrumentalised by the Bretton Woods institutions and the Washington consensus to make it the preserve of technocrats, while excluding citizens from shaping public policies. The paper proposes an alternative reading based on historical analysis of everyday democracy and democratic struggles in Africa and the nature of the social contract, noting also that democracy cannot be fully understood without an analysis of how it responds to the concerns of citizens. It is emphasised that a new understanding of democratic governance and accountability requires the study of Africa on its own terms, avoiding a stylised reading of Africa against the background of an ideal form of democracy in other regions of the world. The radical analysis in this paper is an important intervention in the understanding of democratisation in Africa and a reference point for scholars, policy-makers, media practitioners and activists with an interest in the momentum for change in Africa.

Cyril Obi
Senior Researcher
The Nordic Africa Institute

Democratic Governance and Accountability in Africa: In search of a workable framework

Over the last two decades, Africa has witnessed major momentum. Although I would not go as far as calling it momentum for democratisation, I would certainly characterise the current situation as initial momentum for political reform and change on the continent. In the early 1990s, we began to witness movements that would crystallise in different parts of the continent, culminating in some cases, beginning with Benin, in the sovereign national conferences that were convened to try to change the rules of the political game in many of our countries. It was also during this period that there occurred perhaps one of the most intensive moments in the postcolonial African history of constitution-making, rewriting of constitutions and reform to electoral systems in order to usher in a new era of democratic governance on the continent.

The sources of the pressures that produced the momentum and the movement for political reform have been debated extensively in the literature (Olukoshi 2005:178-84). I will not spend much time on the debates themselves. There were those who argued that political reform was the result of predominantly internal factors in African countries, while others opined that external pressures were dominant. This paper takes the middle ground and argues that the dialectic of the internal and external produced an excellent conjuncture of factors that produced the change, or at least the pressures for the change, that Africa witnessed and continues to witness.

It is important to recall that soon after independence African countries, almost all of which achieved sovereignty on the basis of multiparty governance, soon dissolved into single party and military regimes. Such single party regimes were often justified on several grounds, including the diversities of African countries and the complexities associated with managing them, such that it would be better for the countries of the continent to unite behind a single political project. The same argument was extended to justify military rule in some ways, and both military and single party rule came to be further underpinned by arguments that development and the need for Africa to catch up quickly required nothing less than the harnessing of all national energies behind a single political project.

One of the intellectual partisans of the 1960s, Joseph Ki-Zerbo, made fun of such arguments in favour of single party rule in the 1970s and 1980s. He was one of the few intellectuals among the early titans of African nationalism and played a part right from the beginning of the postwar struggles for independence, which also involved Nkrumah, Kenyatta and others, through to the 1960s. He then went into the university world, and witnessed a gradual process after independence whereby the effervescence of change was gradually sacrificed on the altar of development (Ki-Zerbo 1992; Badim 1999:615-627; CODESRIA Bul-

letin 2007). He remarked that when he visited state houses to see former friends
with whom he had manned the barricades, he would be welcomed symbolically
by big signs proclaiming "Silence! Development in Progress." These words, he
felt, symbolised the period, both in the sense of the determination to accelerate
development on the continent, but more so in erroneously seeking to achieve
this by undermining political pluralism across the continent.

The concern was that diversity needed not to be recognised and woven into
the political system as ingredients for its democratisation. Rather, a premium was
placed on squeezing political diversity out of the system, even suppressing and denying it in order to achieve an integrated political order that would allow greater
national unity and facilitate the task of nation-building (Olukoshi 2002:14-16).
It was a very seductive set of considerations, considering that colonialism itself
had been built on divide and rule, which mobilised ethno-religious and regional
differences to sustain itself. In the order of things across the continent during
the era of colonial rule, certain ethnic groups were considered suitable for military service and recruited accordingly, while others were considered to have the
administrative acumen needed to support the colonial administration. Still others were considered talented traders who would play a key role in the economy.
These divisions, which effectively coincided with ethno-territorial boundaries,
made the task of postcolonial nation-building much more difficult. The tragedy
in all this was that the single party or military rulers themselves reproduced the
very same divisions and conflicts in the ways in which they constituted their rule,
even though they justified their style of rule on the grounds that it was important
to overcome divisions and conflicts associated with diversity. Single party rulers or military dictatorships in a sense ended up reproducing the domination of
ethno-regional elites and sometimes religious domination in many countries. The
issue of inclusion that was a key argument for dismantling multiparty rule was
translated in practice into a continuing politics of exclusion. This in turn began
to sow the seeds of the conflicts – civil wars in some cases, low intensity conflicts
in others – that most African countries were to experience after independence as
excluded groups protested, rebelled or sought forceful inclusion.

Few of these conflicts translated into secessionist movements, Congo-Kin-
shasa (Democratic Republic of Congo or DRC) being perhaps the best-known
case of secessionist strife. But even where secession was not on the political agenda, conflict and instability constituted one of the main features of postcolonial
political settings in Africa in the 1960s and 1970s. For the countries of West
Africa and Central Africa, that conflict took the form of repeated coups d'état.
Every coup set the stage for the next, to the point where only two of the 16 countries of the West African sub-region had escaped military rule by the end of the
1970s. And one of these, Côte d'Ivoire, would eventually succumb to military
rule and descend into civil war, from which it has yet to fully recover.

The political exclusion, authoritarianism and instability already evident in the first two decades of independence were further compounded by the socioeconomic crisis across African countries in late 1970s and early 1980s. Economic crisis was not a significant issue in the first decade of independence, because of the fairly good growth rates African countries enjoyed at independence. These ranged between 7 and 10 per cent and ranked among the highest in the world, qualifying certain African countries as among the world's best performers. Indeed, countries like Kenya and Ivory Coast were described as being among the economic miracles of the time. More commonplace at the time was the so-called Hindu rate of growth, that is rates of growth above 4 per cent, just above population growth rate and the Indian average during the 1960s and 1970s, while African countries experienced in the first decades of independence growth rates of 6,7 and 8 per cent, and even double-digit growth. On account of this growth, it was possible for the nationalist, anti- colonial coalition that inherited power to deliver on the social pact on the basis of which it had mobilised resistance to continued colonial rule across the continent.

Central to that social pact was access to health and education, as well as the social and class mobility such access to education offered households and even communities, thus allowing them to become an important element in the postcolonial social order. In a sense, this mobility and the prospects it afforded for improvement in livelihoods and economic growth made it easier for governments to adopt an authoritarian course. Once economic crisis set in, with its attendant exclusion and instability, in a context of authoritarianism, resistance was bound to crystallise, especially as the costs of the economic austerity measures introduced to contain the economic crisis of the late 1970s and 1980s were unevenly distributed.

The paper will revert later to the theoretical explanation that has been developed in the literature to capture some of these trends. For now, the analysis focuses on the structure of the austerity measures African governments introduced to stem the crisis that built up in the early 1980s. African governments found themselves with no alternative but to embrace the International Monetary Fund (IMF) and the World Bank and to usher in the structural adjustment era. The dynamics of structural adjustment simply became part and parcel of an already existing economic crisis. In some ways these measures exacerbated the crisis, but they also created new contradictions that, I would argue, combined with existing problems in the polity and in political governance to make the pressure for change simply inevitable. It is in this context that the paper locates the domestic dimension of the pressures for democratisation on the continent (Olukoshi 2002:17). These pressures, when they were eventually managed, almost universally translated into electoral pluralism. The question we need to address is the extent to which we can understand democracy, democratisation and democratic accountability in terms of electoral pluralism and the way in which it has unfolded over the last 20 years across the continent.

Externally, African countries were ushered into the contemporary world system at a time when the East-West Cold War was the dominant issue in international relations. This was a context that at one level played out in favour of independence and autonomy, but at another also acted to subvert both. That double aspect of the Cold War had its worst outcomes again in the DRC, which from the very first day of independence to this day has never known peace or stability worth the name. In other settings, the Cold War context provided the possibilities for global alliances to be struck that ultimately resulted in the independence of the former Portuguese colonies of Mozambique and Angola, even laying the groundwork for intensification of the struggle to dismantle apartheid in South Africa. In sum, the Cold War hampered the management of political change on the African continent. However, by the end of the 1980s, with the rise to power of Mikhail Gorbachev, the collapse of Berlin Wall and the dissolution of the USSR and the Warsaw Pact, the Cold War as we knew it abruptly came to an end and the world was ushered into a new phase of international relations. There was a realignment of forces on a global scale that made it possible for some key powers in the international system, especially the so-called victorious powers in the Cold War, to begin to tell their clients and allies in Africa that the political dictatorship and domination of the crudest type that existed in some countries could no longer be tolerated.

All of this coincided with internal pressures for change, making change inevitable. Even Mobutu found he had to respond to pressures from Washington and elsewhere to introduce political reforms as the price of continued international support for his regime. Wamba dia Wamba, one of the DRC's leading historians, recounts how when the American secretary of state visited Mobutu to observe the progress with political reforms, Mobutu proudly asserted that the DRC (then Zaire) had actually surpassed the US in democratic reform because it had over 60 political parties! Those parties were, however, mostly funded by Mobutu himself: they were "portfolio parties" that lacked significant presence on the ground. But this episode in itself gives us an insight into some of the difficulties Africa has subsequently faced in the transition from authoritarian governance to more democratic forms. The differences between substance and form and the tensions arising from them have crystallised in different ways across the continent. The question arises whether we can actually characterise the transitions that were taking place as "democratic" or capable of delivering democratic governance, a live issue of discussion and debate among scholars, and not an easy question to answer.

One takes the view that even in the most authoritarian regimes it is always possible to identify sources of democratic pressure. Democratic politics do not come to an end simply because an authoritarian regime is in power. If we take the view that democracy is a process in which people not only seek to participate, but also through which to extract accountability from authority and to discipline politics and power in the interest the commons, then of course democracy and democratic struggles constitute a living and an abiding part of any political system. There are no doubt moments when democratic struggles recede, just as there are moments when democratic struggles flourish and boom. The question requiring understanding is what determines the ebbs and the flows in democratic pressures: this is a big research question that scholars have not sufficiently dealt with. We often take a pro-forma approach to understanding democracy and democratic politics by seeking to measure what we see and observe on the ground against the performance of what we perceive and conceptualise as an ideal model of democracy. If democratic politics constitutes an abiding part of everyday experience and the processes which we began to witness at the end of the 1980s across Africa in which pressures for reform built up and crystallised into open struggle and open challenges to authority and political change, then perhaps we could argue that the worst attempt towards resurgence in democratic forms of participation was borne out of frustration that accumulated over a period of at least two decades of political crisis and instability. It also flowed from mass disillusionment following a period of economic crisis and social decay that we witnessed in the 1980s as the structural adjustment programme began to bite across the continent.

Scholars have been divided in their assessments of the quality of the change that has occurred. On the one hand there are those who describe themselves as Afro-optimists. A friend, a scholar, once said that this school, strongest within the Diaspora, basically proclaims, "Africa! Africa! Africa! No matter what, Africa!" and seeks to squeeze drops of hope out of even situations of utter hopelessness. This school differs radically from those scholars who take the view that nothing good will come out of the continent. These are the two extremes, often looming larger in journalistic interpretations than in scholarly analysis. Between them is a spectrum of views and perspectives which may have degrees of truth to them, but which also add considerably to the conceptual and theoretical confusion in our understanding of the struggles for democracy and democratic accountability on the continent.

Scholars such as Claude Ake, for example, argued that the problem with the transition Africa witnessed in the late 1980s and the 1990s was precisely that it was anchored in a liberal understanding of democracy. The transition tried to mimic models of liberal democracy imported from the US and Europe, which ultimately delivered on the ground in Africa a democracy that essentially comprised "voting without choosing" (Ake 1994, 1996). The scholar Lisa Laakso (1999) tried to test Ake's model for interpreting and understanding the transitional process in her thesis on Zimbabwe, a widely celebrated and cited study.

Others argued that it was too much to expect that the transition Africa was going through would deliver the kind of democratic outcomes evident in the West, precisely because the conditions for democratic transition in Africa were simply absent or were not ripe enough. There are very serious scholars who have invested in this line of thinking. What you could realistically expect was a tropicalised version of democracy. In *Africa Works*, Chabal and Daloz argue that chaos and the instrumentalisation of power are the norm in the aggregation of power and influence and the motor that drives politics and change on the African continent (Chabal and Daloz 1999). Others argued that the problem with democratic transition was that the continent in which democracy was being built was without bearers of the democratic project – democracy without democrats, to use shorthand. Even where civil society was efflorescent across the continent – which was the case across the board where new forms of associational life flourished – in the end it was a case of an "uncivil" civil society agenda unfolding that could not effectively underwrite the democratic transition.

The arguments are many. Perhaps the most powerful of the criticisms, and easily the most influential academically and in terms of policy consequences, was that of the neo-patrimonial approach, around which a whole political economy developed (Olukoshi 2005:191-4). It essentially argued that power in Africa, organised as it is around neo-patrimonial networks that pervaded all levels of society, simply would make it impossible for Africa to develop the kind of robust democratic change that the transition appeared to have promised. Now, the neo-patrimonial approach itself had been developed much earlier in the political economy of structural adjustment to try to understand why African economies went into crisis in the first place in the late 1970s. It began with the widely cited work by Robert Bates on agriculture in tropical Africa, sometimes supplemented by some of the analysis done by Peter Ekeh on colonialism and the two publics (Ekeh 1975:91-112), not to mention some of the writings by Lipton on the urban bias in African politics (Lipton 1984:139-66, 1989). All these were combined and synthesised into a biased notion of the "politics of the belly" (Bayart 1993) and of the way in which prebends and prebendalism (Joseph 1987) and the sharing of the loot and resources of the continent constituted a key element in the organisation of political life. In that context, it would be impossible for rational economic policy-making to take place and for liberal democracy of the kind that exists or is purported to exist in mature, advanced democracies to be reproduced in Africa.

Much of the existing literature has been trapped in this neo-patrimonial logic. When we consider all the subsequent analyses of the African political, economic and social landscape, they represent different shades and extensions of the notion of neo-patrimonialism. Discussions of aid effectiveness and how to make aid more effective ultimately boil down to how to curb the neo-patrimonial state. Discussions about how to achieve effective governance of economic and political processes are ultimately also reduced to discussions of how to overcome the neo-patrimonial state. That state itself, if it had been able to deliver a modicum of services that would have ensured citizen consent and acquiescence in the governance process, would probably have been considered good enough governance for the African continent. At least, that is what Patrick Chabal and Daloz in their *Africa Works* imply if their analysis is carried to its logical conclusion.

The problem, though, according to people like Callaghy (1984), was that the state in Africa was a neo-patrimonial state which was also increasingly becoming a "lame leviathan," omnipresent but not omnipotent. And even by the end of the 1980s, its omnipresence had been severely undermined by the very logic of the neo-patrimonialism on which it stood, so that continuing to command sufficient loyalty and the consent of those governed became impossible. With dictatorship under military rule or a single party regime no longer an option, it is little wonder that the discordant voices of dissent crystallised at a level where the interplay between greed and grievance became an important element in the political landscape.

Again, we are familiar with the literature on greed and grievance and the arguments of different scholars. Most notably, Paul Collier and others (Collier and Hoeffler 2004:563-95; Collier 2007) attempted to understand the conflicts unleashed across the continent in the wake of the transition or the effort to transit to multiparty politics in terms of the fight over resources, including natural resources of various kinds, and of a political economy of greed and grievance.

The problem with much of the analysis offered in the neo-patrimonial approach of the quest for democracy and accountable governance in Africa is precisely that it is a framework that is omnibus and deterministic and attempts to answer everything using the same single explanatory paradigm. If African economies went into crisis, they did so only because of neo-patrimonialism. If African politics experienced instability, it was also precisely because of the same neo-patrimonial pressures. A universal explanation such as the neo-patrimonial model purported to be ultimately does not enable us to decode the nuances of change and the bearers of change, even when we see them in the field. It is here, I think, that perhaps we get a macro picture of transition that does not allow us to understand the politics of transition and change on the continent or even have a possibility to mobilise them. Because if every aspect of societal life and every layer of society is submitted to a neo-patrimonial logic, where will change come from? And who could be the bearer of change, who is not himself or herself immersed in neo-patrimonial considerations? The neo-patrimonial perspective in many ways is a dead-end analysis that feeds the Afro-pessimism that dominated most scholarly thinking during the 1980s and 1990s and ultimately made it impossible for us to see the potential for democracy in the everyday struggles and adaptations ordinary Africans embarked on in the face of prolonged instability and crisis. Nor should we overlook Africans' resilience in the face of pandemics to produce change in their contexts and livelihoods, or the sparks of popular stirring that need to be supported and built upon in order to produce a democratic form and a democratic transition better adapted to the African context.

How do we get out of this dead-end in our thinking about democratic accountability and governance in Africa? Even if a new neo-patrimonial logic is discovered, many of the political and policy practices associated with it have become embedded in practices on the continent and need to unpacked one after the other. During the structural adjustment years, the notion of "good governance" was introduced as one of the panaceas for achieving effective economic reform on the continent and for helping to underwrite the processes of political transition that were beginning to take place. Up to that point, the World Bank, even though it was heavily immersed in politics and in the politics of economic reform, had taken the view that its constitution and rules prevented it from dabbling in political questions. However, with the introduction of the notion of good governance it was able for the first time to openly engage with political institutions and political questions. But there was difficulty in defining exactly what the notion could be extended to, even including defining what a good governance system is or could be. The notion of good governance was subordinated in the first instance to the larger project of how to save the structural adjustment project itself. After a decade of implementing structural adjustment and of the difficulties in getting results out of it, the search was on for what could be the missing link that could make adjustment deliver the results the authors of the programme promised in the first place. Thus, African countries appeared to be mired in deeper crisis and new contradictions appeared to have developed, even in countries defined as good adjusters that had accepted all the IMF's and World Bank's prescriptions.

Governance in this sense became instrumentalised in the hands of the Bretton Woods institutions to serve not necessarily democracy but the economics of the reform agenda, that was itself questioned on the grounds that it was anti-democratic. It is little wonder that when pressed to decode how good governance would translate in practical terms, the Bank and the UNDP and others ultimately came to define good governance in terms of property rights, the rule of law, judicial independence, transparency and all of the things we are familiar withs. Upon close examination, it can be seen that the investments made in good governance were basically to strengthen the environment for business. They were also intended to strengthen the capacity of the Bretton Woods institutions to have access to information from governments and make them transparent in order to be able to carry out their intervention in the African countries. Good governance is clearly not an option, because it is not democratic governance. It was probably never meant to be equated with democratic governance. The view, again influenced by the neo-patrimonial model, that perhaps we needed to find ways of insulating policy-makers from the day-to-day pressures of politics then subsequently took hold across the continent as an alternative, perhaps even extension, of the good governance logic.

Policy-making was said to be a sphere to capture by vested interest groups and powerful interests, many of which are still embedded in neo-patrimonial models of accumulation, dependent on the state and on privileged access to state resources as a way of consolidating their power and influence. For policy-making to be rational and to take in the best interest of the commons, it must be insulated from the pressures of such interest groups and embody the technocratic logic said to be instrumental in the transformation of some of the more developed countries. This became the key project of the 1990s. Studies, including by United Nations Research Institute for Social Development (UNRISD), have shown that what this translated into in practice was the removal of whole swathes of the policy arena from the purview of elected governments and parliaments (Gibbon, Bangura and Ofstad 1992; Olukoshi 2005), and its placement in the hands of technocrats accountable only to transnational power represented by the Bretton Woods institutions.

In places like Uganda, almost all of East Africa, where reforms on land and access to and use of land were pursued vigorously, those reforms were not subject to domestic debate or to effective parliamentary scrutiny, despite the fact that legislation was being pushed through to effect the change desired. The power of the ministries of finance, the so-called independence of the central bank, whose governors were appointed (most of them incidentally being seconded from the IMF or the World Bank) to positions not open to scrutiny and for which they could not be called to account either by public opinion or even by elected governments, constituted the effective making of a technocracy and of the associated insulation of policy and public officials. This was perhaps one of the most anti-democratic experiences of the 1990s across African continent, whose consequences continued to play out in terms of the nature and form of policy-making on the continent.

Clearly, we cannot talk meaningfully about democratic governance and accountability if citizens cannot take an active part in policy-making and be confident that their active citizenry will help shape public policy. This is precisely the scenario in Africa today, a scenario Thandika Mkandawire has described as a case of Africa having choice-less democracies (Mkandawire 1996). This is a situation in which policy on key issues in the economy and society or social processes are completely out of the realm of public discussion and belong to a technocratic policy elite very much tied to a transnational power structure basically organised around the Washington consensus, with all its difficulties.

I would add that a further dimension of *technocratisation* was achieved in or unwittingly delivered to Africa by the efforts to manage the conflicts and crisis that developed across the continent in the wake of the Cold War.

What Mary Kaldor described as Africa's 'new wars' arose from or resulted in the collapse of central governmental authority in places like Somalia, Sierra Leone and, for a period, Algeria, even to some extent in Liberia. In places like Guinea-Bissau, where effective central governmental authority was eroded over time, the ability to control national territorial space was called into question, giving room for the emergence of the humanitarian-intervention, peace-building and conflict-resolution machinery principally involving the UN. It also involved an army of NGOs built around the peace and security industry, which made for security-sector reform and the restoration of peace, with peace-building as one of the key complements to the processes of economic reform and political engineering taking place on the continent. For countries where military rule had been prolonged and where the quest for elected governance was strong, suggestions such as the subordination of the military to elected governmental authority constituted a welcome development, because this was precisely an issue over which struggles had been waged in countries such as Nigeria and others that have experienced prolonged post-independence military interventions after independence.

But security sector reforms also easily became a set of technical prescriptions, very much like the reforms in the economy and the technocratisation of the policy process. Politics was emptied out of security, just as politics was emptied out of economic policy-making and management on the continent. How would Africa be able to build democratic governance if either we emptied politics out of policy or considered politics to be a problem, an obstacle? As Larry Summers, chief economist of the World Bank actually observed, we have reached a point in the world where in many ways democratic politics was becoming an obstacle to rational economic policy-making, and that it would be necessary to find ways of disciplining politics effectively. We have seen the ascendancy of a particular brand of economics to which even we non-economists respond by beginning to quantify our political science, our sociology, to make it look and sound more like economics. This we do under the pressures associated with the technocratisation of policy thinking and policy-making in a direction that strips politics out of our thinking and out of the solutions Africa seeks. I have no problem with quantification in the social sciences and I think no social science is complete which does not adopt a degree of quantification to capture trends and processes. But quantification such as that undertaken to date on the basis of short-run temporal data as opposed to long-term material that enables us to establish trends certainly has to be avoided.

Perhaps the starting point is to begin to rediscover our sense of historical analysis and the importance of situating processes and trends relating to democracy and governance within a long-run analysis of historical trends and unfolding processes. Too often, short-term developments and trends are captured and verdicts are given under the pressures of the new media age we inhabit that suggest a conclusion even before the drama is over. And here we can cite the example of the election conflict in Kenya. If you look at the analysis when that conflict was occurring and at the analysis of post-referendum Kenya, you will find that sometimes the same commentators came to widely different conclusions, forgetting that three, four years before some had said "this was the end of Kenya, democracy doesn't work for Africa. It's the kind of conflict and violence that we predicted would happen because of the diversities that we deal with." And yet today we are told that, given all the lessons the political actors have drawn from that experience, maybe Kenya is finally beginning to overcome ethnic divisions and moving towards a new era of democracy and democratisation in its postcolonial history. The importance of being able to do long-run analysis is to enable us to avoid some of those easy, perhaps flippant conclusions, of which the likes of Paul Collier and his co-travellers have the economic data and intelligence to do their analysis and minister to very urgent donor demands for policy-relevant material. Such analysis then form the core of policy-prescriptions that they can use immediately to intervene in failed states or failing states whose fragility might threaten the peace and stability of many of our countries or even of the international community.

History, I can never underscore enough, is an important prerequisite for an understanding of democracy at an analytical and conceptual level. But it is also important to rediscover ourselves, our dialectics, because we seem also to have settled into a world in which somehow things have to happen in a natural and progressive order, in a cumulative unidirectional way, in an incrementalism that can only be upwards, as though change in society, in any society, follows a path that is unilinear, straight and straightforward. In fact, change is always complicated, occurs sometimes in ways that are imperceptible. The need, therefore, is for us in our dialectics to pay more attention to everyday democracy and democratic struggles – to the kinds of struggles people engage in, for instance, with the police; to the kind of encounters cross-border traders have with custom officials in negotiating relations that make it possible for them to carry out their trade; to the informal sectors and the way in which they make their own contribution to processes of adaptation and change. These are the kinds of issues that will be categorised as low-level political issues, but which are so central to everyday life. But by focusing on high-level issues of security sector reform, democratic consolidation, of indexes of transparency such as Mo Ibrahim's on governance indicators (Ibrahim Index of African Governance 2010), useful though these macro-issues are, we sometimes fail to discover the dialectics of change and how it is articulated in many of our societies.

So let us rediscover our dialectics and understand that it is out of contradiction that change is produced. Democracy will not be democracy if it is not underpinned by struggle and it is out of the struggles among groups over their interests that democracy is produced. If the conflict in Kenya, regrettable though the loss of lives and mindless violence were, did not take place, perhaps the constitutional reform celebrated today would not have come about. Nobody could perhaps have predicted the outcome, but the issue of constitutional reform in Kenya has been on the cards for a very long time. Even the idea of forming a government that would work towards a new constitution represented one of the solutions negotiated after the post-election crisis. But the struggles that needed to be undertaken – sometimes violent, sometimes hidden, sometimes subterranean – are an important element that we need always to build into our analysis and understanding of change.

A third issue we need to take note of is that ultimately democratic politics will not make complete sense if the state and the state system is not itself robust. The structural adjustment programme was devoted to rolling back the frontiers of the state. Many on the left, including myself, have spent a lifetime fighting the state in different forms and in different ways. But let us not mistakenly assume that one can ever build a society on a democratic footing without having an effective and functioning state system in the first place. Indeed, part of the democratic struggle is precisely how to build such a functioning and effective state that responds to the concerns of the commons as opposed to simply serving the interests of a narrow class and elite group that often dominates its affairs. Scholars like Thandika Mkandawire (2001), Yusuf Bangura (2006), Omano Edigheji (2010) and the like have been reflecting on precisely the rebuilding of a democratic developmental state in Africa and have invested huge intellectual resources in this effort to restore the state itself and its functionality in Africa.

Beyond recognising the importance of the state, we also need to understand that in every political order and system there must always be a bargain involved in being a member of that political community. The question we must ask ourselves is what the bargain is for the ordinary African today in being a member of a political community? What does it mean to be Senegalese? What does it mean to be a Nigerian? This is the arena of citizenship, the arena of the articulation of the relationship between state and society. It is an arena suffused with informal relationships but also an arena where formalised social contracts become an essential ingredient of the political society. We cannot understand or even begin to theorise governance and accountability if we do not have a sense of the nature of the social contract in any given political system. Because it is within the social contract, within the bargain that makes me a member of a political community, that I seek accountability as a member of that political community and also seek to exercise my active citizenship. So, again, why don't we rediscover issues of how people in their everyday struggles articulate demands on the state through a set of expectations that they have in order to make it more accountable? When, today, we go to Africa and ask people what do you make of two decades of multiparty politics in your country?, people say, "Well, we are still waiting for the dividends of democracy." We need to understand that they are actually speaking of the absence of the social bargain that is a key element in the glue that makes democracies function and the system reproduce itself on the basis of legitimacy and be able to achieve the kind of consent that is necessary.

Next, and perhaps even more difficult for us working on democratic questions, is the fact that perhaps Africa has lost ground, maybe too much ground, with regard to policy-making on the continent. Policy-making, policy process and policy institutions have not only been captured, but hijacked to a point where rulers on the ground essentially exercise power, but the determinants of policy appear to be extraverted and external to the continent. This process started with structural adjustment, the Washington consensus, but is one that has even been extended beyond structural adjustment to core areas of social and economic policy such as Poverty Reduction Strategic Papers, the Millennium Development Goals, and increasingly, even democratisation. There is no shortage of those indexes and indices, from Freedom House to Transparency International and beyond, producing reports every year that essentially seek to measure the state of democracy and democratisation in many of our countries.

All of the foregoing has added to the erosion of the domestic policy space and domestic policy processes. Rebuilding the state and rebuilding an agenda for the consolidation of a properly functioning state in Africa would inevitably include revisiting the policy process and policy institutions across the continent to ensure that domestic policy processes are restored in a way that will allow for the engagement of the citizenry. A French newspaper editorial a decade ago lamented that in France ministers would, in response to questions about why they had adopted certain policies, argue that it was not their fault – they were still loyal French politicians and citizens – but the fault of globalisation. Essentially, what we have seen in Africa over the last two decades is governments basically denying responsibility for policy and simply either saying that they are following global trends or have to respond to demands from outside the continent from an assortment of donors. How do we rebuild policy space and the politics around policy-making on the continent? It seems that the solution will not only depend on the quality of citizenship, but also on decision-making that would enable us to further consolidate democracy on our continent.

In conclusion, it is important to reiterate that most analysis of the processes of change in Africa continues to be informed by a stylised reading of what is considered to be classical experience in other regions of the world. This is social science, as it were, by analogy, in which Africa is not read in terms of its own internal dynamics and processes, of what is going on, on its own terms. Ultimately, societies make change through a process of learning and learning is cumulative. And accumulated learning enables people not to repeat some of the errors and mistakes of a previous generation, at least not in the same way. But I do not believe that the kind of learning implied in much of the social science by analogy, not least in the literature on neo-patrimonialism, that begins with a stylised presentation of a supposedly ideal model based on what's supposedly happened or is happening in one region of the world, mainly Europe and North America, can be applied to the African context. This approach has certainly run its course.

Therefore, it would be useful for us to begin to pull out of the African experience the kinds of lessons that will enrich ongoing debates and extend the frontiers of knowledge. This approach would enable us to strengthen the discussion and debate on democratic governance and accountability in a way that would probably allow us to do genuinely comparative politics for the first time and enhance our understanding of comparative experiences. No two democracies are equal, no two democracies are the same. There might be similarities and there are features that distinguish democracies from non-democratic forms of governance. Nevertheless, every democracy has a specific history, a specific dialectic. There are spoken and unspoken norms that define the bodies politic of every country and which make the metaphors of discussion and exchange intelligible to the members of that political community. Let us seek to understand Africa on its own terms, in terms of its own dynamics, in a way that can enable us to take the African experience into the global arena of comparison to produce a truly comparative theory of democratisation on a world scale. This is what all of us have yearned for for a very long time and this is what the Gulbenkian Commission says is within our reach.

Bibliography

Ake, Claude, 1994, "The Democratisation of Disempowerment in Africa", *CASS Occasional Monograph* . Lagos: Malthouse.

—, 1996, *Democracy and Development in Africa*. Washington DC: Brookings Institution.

Badim, Amade, 1999, "Joseph Ki-Zerbo (1922–)," *Prospects: The quarterly review of comparative education* XXIX, 4, 1999, pp. 615–27.

Bangura, Yusuf and George Larbi (eds), 2006, *Public Sector Reforms in Developing Countries.* Hampshire: Palgrave Macmillan.

Bayart, Jean-Francis, 1993, *The State in Africa: Politics of the Belly.* London: Longmans.

Bratton, Michael and Nicholas van der Walle, 1994, "Neo-patrimonial regimes and political transitions in Africa," *World Politics* 46.

Callaghy, Thomas , 1984, *The state-society struggle: Zaire in contemporary perspective.* New York: Columbia University Press.

Chabal, Pascal and Jean-Pascal Daloz, 1999, *Africa Works: Disorder as Political Instrument.* London, Oxford and Bloomington: International African Institute with James Currey and Indiana University Press.

CODESRIA Bulletin, Nos. 3 and 4, 2007.

Collier, Paul , 2007, *The Bottom Billion.* Oxford: Oxford University Press.

— and Anke Hoeffler, 2004, "Greed and Grievance in Civil Wars," *Oxford Economic Papers* 56, 4.

Edigheji, Omano (ed.), 2010, *Constructing a Democratic Developmental State in South Africa.* Pretoria: Human Sciences Research Council.

Ekeh, Peter, 1975, "Colonialism and the Two Publics in Africa: A Theoretical Statement," *Comparative Studies in Politics and History* 17, 1.

Gibbon, Peter, Yusuf Bangura and Arve Ofstad, 1992, *Authoritarianism, Democracy and Adjustment: The politics of economic reform in Africa.* Uppsala: Nordiska Afrikainstitutet.

Ibrahim Index of African Governance 2010, http://www.moibrahimfoundation.org/en/section/the-ibrahim-index (accessed 25 April 2011).

Joseph, Richard , 1987, *Democracy and Prebendal Politics in Nigeria: The Rise and Fall of the Second Republic.* Cambridge: Cambridge University Press.

Ki-Zerbo, Joseph , 1992, *La natte des autres (pour un développement endogène en Afrique)* [Other people's mats (for an endogenous development in Africa)]. Proceedings of the symposium of the Research Centre for Endogenous Development (CRDE), Bamako, 1989. Paris, CODESRIA/Karthala.

Laakso, Lisa , 1999, *Voting Without Choosing: State Making and Elections in Zimbabwe,* Acta Politica No. 11, Department of Political Science, University of Helsinki.

Lipton, Michael, 1977, *Why Poor People Stay Poor: Urban Bias in the World.* Aldershot: Avebury.

—, 1984, "Urban bias revisted", *Journal of Development Studies* 20, 3.

Mamdani, Mahmoud, Thandika Mkandawire and Ernest Wamba dia Wamba (eds), 1988, *Social Movements, Social Transformation and the Struggle for Democracy in Africa*. Dakar: CODESRIA.

Mkandawire, Thandika, 1999, "Crisis Management and the Making of Choiceless Democracies" in Joseph, Richard (ed.), *State, Conflict and Democracy in Africa*. London: Lynne Rienner.

—, 2001, "Thinking About Development States in Africa," *Cambridge Journal of Economics* 25, 3.

— and Adebayo Olukoshi (eds), 1996, *Between Liberalization and Oppression: The Politics of Structural Adjustment in Africa*, Dakar: CODESRIA.

Adebayo Olukoshi, 1998, *The Elusive Prince of Denmark: Structural Adjustment and the Politics of Governance in Africa*. Uppsala: Nordiska Afrikainstitutet.

—, 2002, *Governing the African Developmental Process: The Challenge of the New Partnership for Africa's Development*. Copenhagen: Centre for African Studies Occasional Paper, September 2002.

—, 2005, "Changing patterns of politics in Africa", in Boron, Atilio and Gladys Lechini (eds), *Politics and Social Movements in an Hegemonic World*. Buenos Aires: CLASCO.

Wamba-dia-Wamba, Ernest , 1992,"Beyond Elite Politics in Africa," *Quest* 6, 1.

DISCUSSION PAPERS PUBLISHED BY THE INSTITUTE

Recent issues in the series are available electronically for download free of charge
www.nai.uu.se

1. Kenneth Hermele and Bertil Odén, *Sanctions and Dilemmas. Some Implications of Economic Sanctions against South Africa.* 1988. 43 pp. ISBN 91-7106-286-6

2. Elling Njål Tjønneland, *Pax Pretoriana. The Fall of Apartheid and the Politics of Regional Destabilisation.* 1989. 31 pp. ISBN 91-7106-292-0

3. Hans Gustafsson, Bertil Odén and Andreas Tegen, *South African Minerals. An Analysis of Western Dependence.* 1990. 47 pp. ISBN 91-7106-307-2

4. Bertil Egerö, *South African Bantustans. From Dumping Grounds to Battlefronts.* 1991. 46 pp. ISBN 91-7106-315-3

5. Carlos Lopes, *Enough is Enough! For an Alternative Diagnosis of the African Crisis.* 1994. 38 pp. ISBN 91-7106-347-1

6. Annika Dahlberg, *Contesting Views and Changing Paradigms.* 1994. 59 pp. ISBN 91-7106-357-9

7. Bertil Odén, *Southern African Futures. Critical Factors for Regional Development in Southern Africa.* 1996. 35 pp. ISBN 91-7106-392-7

8. Colin Leys and Mahmood Mamdani, *Crisis and Reconstruction – African Perspectives.* 1997. 26 pp. ISBN 91-7106-417-6

9. Gudrun Dahl, *Responsibility and Partnership in Swedish Aid Discourse.* 2001. 30 pp. ISBN 91-7106-473-7

10. Henning Melber and Christopher Saunders, *Transition in Southern Africa – Comparative Aspects.* 2001. 28 pp. ISBN 91-7106-480-X

11. *Regionalism and Regional Integration in Africa.* 2001. 74 pp. ISBN 91-7106-484-2

12. Souleymane Bachir Diagne, et al., *Identity and Beyond: Rethinking Africanity.* 2001. 33 pp. ISBN 91-7106-487-7

13. Georges Nzongola-Ntalaja, et al., *Africa in the New Millennium.* Edited by Raymond Suttner. 2001. 53 pp. ISBN 91-7106-488-5

14. *Zimbabwe's Presidential Elections 2002.* Edited by Henning Melber. 2002. 88 pp. ISBN 91-7106-490-7

15. Birgit Brock-Utne, *Language, Education and Democracy in Africa.* 2002. 47 pp. ISBN 91-7106-491-5

16. Henning Melber et al., *The New Partnership for Africa's development (NEPAD).* 2002. 36 pp. ISBN 91-7106-492-3

17. Juma Okuku, *Ethnicity, State Power and the Democratisation Process in Uganda.* 2002. 42 pp. ISBN 91-7106-493-1

18. Yul Derek Davids, et al., *Measuring Democracy and Human Rights in Southern Africa.* Compiled by Henning Melber. 2002. 50 pp. ISBN 91-7106-497-4

19. Michael Neocosmos, Raymond Suttner and Ian Taylor, *Political Cultures in Democratic South Africa.* Compiled by Henning Melber. 2002. 52 pp. ISBN 91-7106-498-2

20. Martin Legassick, *Armed Struggle and Democracy. The Case of South Africa.* 2002. 53 pp. ISBN 91-7106-504-0

21. Reinhart Kössler, Henning Melber and Per Strand, *Development from Below. A Namibian Case Study.* 2003. 32 pp. ISBN 91-7106-507-5

22. Fred Hendricks, *Fault-Lines in South African Democracy. Continuing Crises of Inequality and Injustice.* 2003. 32 pp. ISBN 91-7106-508-3

23. Kenneth Good, *Bushmen and Diamonds. (Un) Civil Society in Botswana.* 2003. 39 pp. ISBN 91-7106-520-2

24. Robert Kappel, Andreas Mehler, Henning Melber and Anders Danielson, *Structural Stability in an African Context.* 2003. 55 pp. ISBN 91-7106-521-0

25. Patrick Bond, *South Africa and Global Apartheid. Continental and International Policies and Politics.* 2004. 45 pp. ISBN 91-7106-523-7

26. Bonnie Campbell (ed.), *Regulating Mining in Africa. For whose benefit?* 2004. 89 pp. ISBN 91-7106-527-X

27. Suzanne Dansereau and Mario Zamponi, *Zimbabwe – The Political Economy of Decline.* Compiled by Henning Melber. 2005. 43 pp. ISBN 91-7106-541-5

28. Lars Buur and Helene Maria Kyed, *State Recogni-tion of Traditional Authority in Mozambique. The nexus of Community Representation and State Assist-ance.*
2005. 30 pp. ISBN 91-7106-547-4

29. Hans Eriksson and Björn Hagströmer, *Chad – Towards Democratisation or Petro-Dictatorship?*
2005. 82 pp.ISBN 91-7106-549-

30. Mai Palmberg and Ranka Primorac (eds), *Skinning the Skunk – Facing Zimbabwean Futures.*
2005. 40 pp. ISBN 91-7106-552-0

31. Michael Brüntrup, Henning Melber and Ian Taylor, *Africa, Regional Cooperation and the World Market – Socio-Economic Strategies in Times of Global Trade Regimes.* Com-piled by Henning Melber.
2006. 70 pp. ISBN 91-7106-559-8

32. Fibian Kavulani Lukalo, *Extended Handshake or Wrestling Match? – Youth and Urban Culture Celebrating Politics in Kenya.*
2006.58 pp. ISBN 91-7106-567-9

33. Tekeste Negash, *Education in Ethiopia: From Crisis to the Brink of Collapse.*
2006. 55 pp. ISBN 91-7106-576-8

34. Fredrik Söderbaum and Ian Taylor (eds) *Micro-Regionalism in West Africa. Evidence from Two Case Studies.*
2006. 32 pp. ISBN 91-7106-584-9

35. Henning Melber (ed.), *On Africa – Scholars and African Studies.*
2006. 68 pp. ISBN 978-91-7106-585-8

36. Amadu Sesay, *Does One Size Fit All? The Sierra Leone Truth and Reconciliation Commission Revisited.*
2007. 56 pp. ISBN 978-91-7106-586-5

37. Karolina Hulterström, Amin Y. Kamete and Henning Melber, *Political Opposition in African Countries – The Case of Kenya, Namibia, Zambia and Zimbabwe.*
2007. 86 pp. ISBN 978-7106-587-2

38. Henning Melber (ed.), *Governance and State Delivery in Southern Africa. Examples from Botswana, Namibia and Zimbabwe.*
2007. 65 pp. ISBN 978-91-7106-587-2

39. Cyril Obi (ed.), *Perspectives on Côte d'Ivoire: Between Political Breakdown and Post-Conflict Peace.*
2007. 66 pp. ISBN 978-91-7106-606-6

40. Anna Chitando, *Imagining a Peaceful Society. A Vision of Children's Literature in a Post-Conflict Zimbabwe.*
2008. 26 pp. ISBN 978-91-7106-623-7

41. Olawale Ismail, *The Dynamics of Post-Conflict Reconstruction and Peace Building in West Africa. Between Change and Stability.*
2009.52 pp. ISBN 978-91-7106-637-4

42. Ron Sandrey and Hannah Edinger, *Examining the South Africa–China Agricultural Relationship.*
2009. 58 pp. ISBN 978-91-7106-643-5

43. Xuan Gao, *The Proliferation of Anti-Dumping and Poor Governance in Emerging Economies.*
2009. 41 pp. ISBN 978-91-7106-644-2

44. Lawal Mohammed Marafa, *Africa's Business and Development Relationship with China. Seeking Moral and Capital Values of the Last Economic Frontier.*
2009. xx pp. ISBN 978-91-7106-645-9

45. Mwangi wa Githinji, *Is That a Dragon or an Elephant on Your Ladder? The Potential Impact of China and India on Export Led Growth in African Countries.*
2009. 40 pp. ISBN 978-91-7106-646-6

46. Jo-Ansie van Wyk, *Cadres, Capitalists, Elites and Coalitions. The ANC, Business and Development in South Africa.*
2009. 61 pp. ISBN 978-91-7106-656-5

47. Elias Courson, *Movement for the Emancipation of the Niger Delta (MEND). Political Marginalization, Repression and Petro-Insurgency in the Niger Delta.*2009. 30 pp. ISBN 978-91-7106-657-2

48. Babatunde Ahonsi, *Gender Violence and HIV/ AIDS in Post-Conflict West Africa. Issues and Responses.* 2010.
38 pp. ISBN 978-91-7106-665-7

49. Usman Tar and Abba Gana Shettima, *Endangered Democracy? The Struggle over Secularism and its Implications for Politics and Democracy in Nigeria.*
2010. 21 pp. ISBN 978-91-7106-666-4

50. Garth Andrew Myers, *Seven Themes in African Urban Dynamics.*2010. 28 pp.
ISBN 978-91-7106-677-0

51. Abdoumaliq Simone, *The Social Infrastructures of City Life in Contemporary Africa.*
2010. 33 pp. ISBN 978-91-7106-678-7

52. Li Anshan, *Chinese Medical Cooperation in Africa. With Special Emphasis on the Medical Teams and Anti-Malaria Campaign.*
2011. 24 pp. ISBN 978-91-7106-683-1

53. Folashade Hunsu, *Zangbeto: Navigating the Spaces Between Oral art, Communal Security And Conflict Mediation in Badagry, Nigeria.*
2011. 27 pp. ISBN 978-91-7106-688-6

54. Jeremiah O. Arowosegbe, *Reflections on the Challenge of Reconstructing Post-Conflict States in West Africa: Insights from Claude Ake's Political Writings.*
    2011. 40 pp. ISBN 978-91-7106-689-3

55. Bertil Odén, *The Africa Policies of Nordic Countries and the Erosion of the Nordic Aid Model: A comparative study.*
    2011. 66 pp. ISBN 978-91-7106-691-6

56. Angela Meyer, *Peace and Security Cooperation in Central Africa: Developments, Challenges and Prospects.*
    2011. 47 pp ISBN 978-91-7106-693-0

57. Godwin R. Murunga, *Spontaneous or Premeditated? Post-Election Violence in Kenya.*
    2011. 58 pp. ISBN 978-91-7106-694-7

58. David Sebudubudu & Patrick Molutsi, *The Elite as a Critical Factor in National Development: The Case of Botswana.*
    2011. 48 pp. ISBN 978-91-7106-695-4

59. Sabelo J. Ndlovu-Gatsheni, *The Zimbabwean Nation-State Project. A Historical Diagnosis of Identity and Power-Based Conflicts in a Postcolonial State.*
    2011. 97 pp. ISBN 978-91-7106-696-1

60. Jide Okeke, *Why Humanitarian Aid in Darfur is not a Practice of the 'Responsibility to Protect'.*
    2011. 45 pp. ISBN 978-91-7106-697-8

61. Florence Odora Adong, *Recovery and Development Politics. Options for Sustainable Peacebuilding in Northern Uganda.*
    2011, 72 pp. ISBN 978-91-7106-698-5

62. Osita A. Agbu, *Ethnicity and Democratisation in Africa. Challenges for Politics and Development.*
    2011, 30 pp. ISBN 978-91-7106-699-2

63. Cheryl Hendricks, *Gender and Security in Africa. An Overview.*
    2011, 32 pp. ISBN 978-91-7106-700-5

64. Adebayo O. Olukoshi, *Democratic Governance and Accountability in Africa. In Search of a Workable Framework.*
    2011, 25 pp. ISBN 978-91-7106-701-2

www.ingramcontent.com/pod-product-compliance
Lightning Source LLC
Chambersburg PA
CBHW080210300326
41934CB00039B/3448